HAL•LEONARD
INSTRUMENTAL
PLAY-ALONG

AUDIO
ACCESS
INCLUDED

PLAYBACK+
Speed • Pitch • Balance • Loop

VIOLA

A NEW MUSICAL
WICKED

To access audio visit:
www.halleonard.com/mylibrary
Enter Code
1113-3856-1091-4437

ISBN: 978-1-4234-4974-4

HAL•LEONARD®
CORPORATION
7777 W. BLUEMOUND RD. P.O. BOX 13819 MILWAUKEE, WI 53213

Visit Hal Leonard Online at
www.halleonard.com

AS LONG AS YOU'RE MINE

Music and Lyrics by
STEPHEN SCHWARTZ

VIOLA

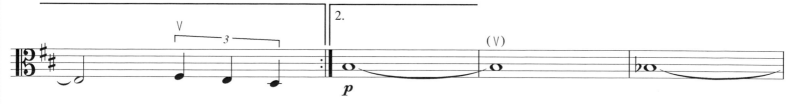

DANCING THROUGH LIFE

VIOLA

Words and Music by
STEPHEN SCHWARTZ

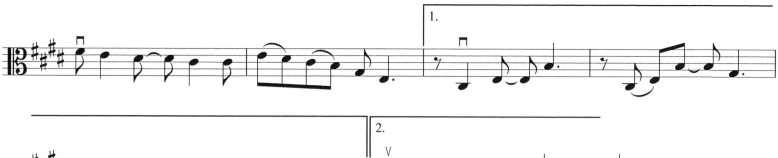

DEFYING GRAVITY

VIOLA

Words and Music by
STEPHEN SCHWARTZ

Allegro, as before

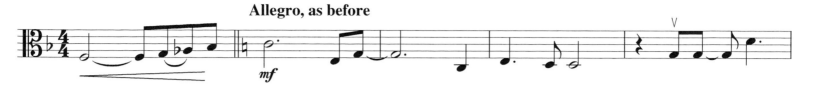

Slower

FOR GOOD

VIOLA

Words and Music by
STEPHEN SCHWARTZ

Più mosso

rit.   *a tempo*

senza rit.

mp

rit. poco a poco

rit.   *a tempo*   *rit.*

I COULDN'T BE HAPPIER

VIOLA

Words and Music by
STEPHEN SCHWARTZ

I'M NOT THAT GIRL

VIOLA

Words and Music by
STEPHEN SCHWARTZ

Simple and steady
Harp

Play

p

To Coda

$(\eighthnote = \eighthnote)$

mf

D.S. al Coda

CODA

poco rit. e dim.

2

rit.

NO GOOD DEED

Words and Music by
STEPHEN SCHWARTZ

VIOLA

13

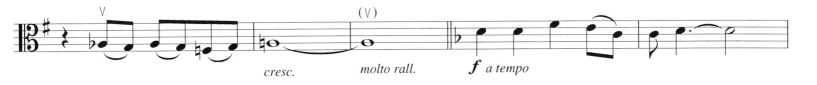

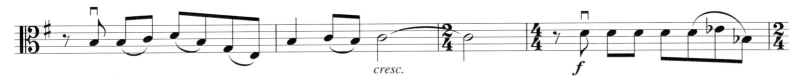

Meno mosso

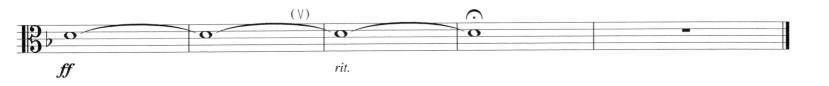

ONE SHORT DAY

VIOLA

Music and Lyrics by
STEPHEN SCHWARTZ

Allegro

poco a poco rit.

Slower   **Tenderly**

a tempo

POPULAR

VIOLA

Words and Music by
STEPHEN SCHWARTZ

WHAT IS THIS FEELING?

Words and Music by
STEPHEN SCHWARTZ

VIOLA

THE WIZARD AND I

VIOLA

Words and Music by
STEPHEN SCHWARTZ

WONDERFUL

VIOLA

Music and Lyrics by
STEPHEN SCHWARTZ

$(\text{♫} = \text{♫})$

rit.

Moderate Ragtime

f

A little slower

rit.   *mp*

molto rit.   *f a tempo*

NO ONE MOURNS THE WICKED

VIOLA

Words and Music by
STEPHEN SCHWARTZ